FISH & SEAFOOD GRILLING

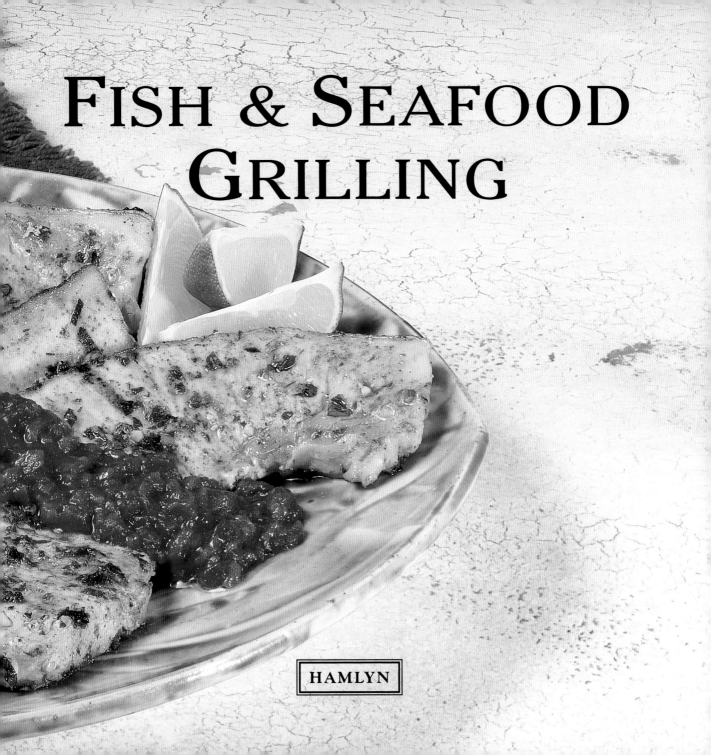

FISH & SEAFOOD GRILLING

HAMLYN

First published in 1998
by Hamlyn
an imprint of Reed Consumer Books Limited
Michelin House, 81 Fulham road, London SW3 6RB
and Auckland, Melbourne and Singapore.

ISBN 0 600 59419 X

Printed in Hong Kong

Photographer: Hilary Moore
Home Economists: Lucy Knox & Sarah Lowman

CONVERSION CHART

Oven Temperatures Recommended Equivalents

°C	°F	Gas Mark
110	225	¼
120	250	½
140	275	1
150	300	2
160	325	3
180	350	4
190	375	5
200	400	6
220	425	7
230	450	8
240	475	9

Conversions from Cups to Imperial and Metric

Solid Measures

American	Imperial and Metric
2 cups butter or margarine	1 lb/500 g
4 cups flour	1 lb/500 g
2 cups granulated or caster sugar	1 lb/500 g
3 cups icing sugar	1 lb/500 g
1 cup rice	8 oz/250 g

Liquid Measures

American	Imperial and Metric
⅔ cup	¼ pint/150 ml
1¼ cups	½ pint/300 ml
2 cups	¾ pint/450 ml
2½ cups	1 pint/600 ml
3¾ cups	1½ pints/900 ml
5 cups	2 pints/1200 ml

Terminology

American	English
Arugula	Rocket
Bell Pepper	Pepper
Eggplant	Aubergine
Cilantro	Coriander
Cookie Sheet	Baking Sheet
Heavy Cream	Double Cream
Light Cream	Single Cream
Plain Flour	All-Purpose Flour
Self-rising Flour	Self-raising Flour
Shrimps	Prawns
Skillet	Frying Pan
Superfine Sugar	Caster Sugar
Sweet Butter	Unsalted Butter
Turbinado Sugar	Demerara Sugar
Zucchini	Courgette

Notes
1 Use whole milk unless otherwise stated. 2 Use sweet (unsalted) butter unless otherwise stated.
3 Use medium-size vegetables unless otherwise stated.

Contents

Fish & Seafood Grilling

Grilling is one of the healthiest and most delicious ways of cooking fish as well as the oldest. Since ancient times, man has enjoyed the wonderful flavors and aromas of fresh fish cooked over an open fire. Crisp and golden on the outside; tender and succulent inside, grilled whole fish or fish fillets is the perfect low-fat food for warm summer days when it can be cooked outside on a barbecue. It is ideal for family meals and impromptu parties, and it can be enjoyed anywhere at any time—in your backyard, at the shore, during the day, or under the stars.

The other good thing about grilling is that it requires only minimum culinary skills and even a novice can be successful. Timing is all-important and it is essential to keep an eye on the grill and not to let the fish overcook, or it will start to flake and fall apart. Just follow these guidelines for success.

Tips for successful grilling

Get the barbecue hot
If using an outdoor charcoal grill, light it about an hour in advance of when you plan to cook so as to give it plenty of time to heat up. When the flames die down, the coals glow red and a dull gray dust forms on them, the barbecue is ready and you can start cooking. If using a gas or an electric grill, turn it on about 5 minutes ahead of cooking.

Be prepared
When barbecuing, always keep two bowls beside you: one of water in case of flare-ups when you need to extinguish the flames; and one of marinade, oil, melted butter, or a sauce for basting the fish while it cooks.

Grilling whole fish
When grilling whole fish, wash and clean the fish (see page 11) and remove the scales. Pat dry with paper towels, then fill the body cavity with fresh herbs or the stuffing of your choice. You can cut off the head, tail, and fins but it is not necessary.

Grilling white fish
It is essential when grilling white fish, whether whole soles or flounder on the bone, white fish fillets and steaks, or fish kebobs to baste it frequently with a marinade, melted butter, or oil and lemon juice to keep it moist and prevent it drying out.

Prepare the grid
To prevent the fish sticking while it is being grilled, you should brush some oil over the grid of the barbecue before adding the fish. Alternatively, you can arrange the fish on a sheet of oiled kitchen foil or in a special foil container which can be placed directly over the hot coals. Use a fish slice to turn the fish over to prevent it breaking up and disintegrating. It is also a good idea to use a separate grid for grilling fish to help prevent adding fishy flavors to meat.

Experiment with marinades

Marinades help to flavor the fish and keep it moist while cooking. Do not throw away any leftover marinade; use it to baste the fish. Alternatively, you can baste with oil or melted butter.

Watch the grill

Always keep an eye on the fish while it is cooking to prevent it burning or becoming overcooked. Too much flame is disastrous and the food could end up a burnt offering of unappetizing charcoal.

Protect yourself

Accidents do happen and it is important to take sensible precautions and protect yourself from flames and heat when grilling. Use oven gloves, long-handled fish slices, and tongs to protect your arms and hands.

Grilling on the bone

Although most fish fillets are suitable for grilling, fish tastes best when it is grilled on the bone. Both oily fish, such as salmon, trout, tuna, and red snapper, and white fish are suitable.

Serve immediately

Grilled fish is always at its best when served really hot and straight away. It cannot be reheated successfully.

The process of grilling

Grilled fish is cooked by being directly exposed to a fierce source of heat. In order to concentrate the flavors within the fish, intense heat is essential and the cooking process should be very fast. The fish is cooked when the skin is crisp and golden, and the flesh is cooked through and separates from the bones without flaking or crumbling.

Plan ahead

To save time and enjoy grilled fish at its best, it always helps to plan ahead. Here are a few useful tips to help you make fish and seafood grilling quick and simple.

- Clean and prepare the fish in advance and store in the refrigerator until required. However, do not store it for longer than overnight — fish is always best eaten when it is fresh.
- Make the marinade ahead and marinate the fish for the required time, until needed.
- You can also make flavored butters and sauces in advance and freeze or refrigerate them until required.

7

Grills, fuel, and equipment

There is a wide range of grills that you can use, whether indoor or outdoor. All barbecue cooking implements need long handles to protect you from the heat and flames.

Built-in grill
This may be an overhead grill at eye or waist level or a grill within your oven. With these grills, you can adjust the distance between the food and the heat source, as well as controlling the intensity of the heat. When grilling indoors, you should have adequate ventilation as grilling can cause a lot of smoke and the aroma of fish cooking tends to linger.

Brazier-type barbecue
This is the most basic type of barbecue, consisting of a shallow bowl or "kettle" in which the charcoal is lit. The air flows over the charcoal while the fish is cooking. These barbecues may have a hood or windshield.

Grill-type barbecue
In this sort of barbecue, air vents allow the air to flow up and through the charcoal while the food is cooking.

Gas barbecue
These barbecues are expensive but ideal for fast grilling as they take only five minutes to heat up, and you have instant heat control, usually with high, medium, and low settings. However, to real outdoor grilling aficionados they smack of cheating and they cannot impart the special, distinctive flavor and aroma of charcoal-grilled food.

Fuel
Charcoal is the normal fuel for outdoor grills, normally in briquet or lump wood form. However, you can also use seasoned, dried hard wood or fruit wood, such as apple.

Hickory chips
Aromatic hickory and mesquite chips can be sprinkled on the fire below the fish to add a characteristic smoky flavor. Most of these chips must be soaked in water before use but you can buy "smoke chips" which require no soaking. You could also try sprinkling fresh herbs on the hot coals.

Long-handled cooking implements
You will need a fish slice and tongs for picking up and turning the fish, and a brush for basting it. You may also find a fish-shaped hinged metal grid useful as this can be placed on the barbecue and will enable you to turn the fish more easily.

Kebob skewers
Fish kebobs are the perfect food for grilling—easily prepared and quickly cooked, they are the perfect fast food for busy cooks. Flat metal skewers tend to be preferable to round ones which can turn over involuntarily while cooking. Always pre-soak wooden skewers in water before use as otherwise they could catch alight if there is a flare-up.

Other equipment
Always wear oven gloves when handling even long-handled forks and tongs to turn and remove food from the grill. And when cooking outdoors, remember to take out a trash bag for all the trash, paper plates, and leftovers.

Flavoring the fish

You can add flavor to fish with savory butters, marinades, sauces, herbs, and spices.

Flavored butters

Adding a knob of savory butter to fish during or after cooking will enhance its natural flavor. The butter can be prepared in advance and then rolled into a sausage shape, wrapped in kitchen foil or waxed paper and chilled or frozen until required. Serve them sliced into rounds. Try adding the following flavorings:

- Minced garlic and herbs
- Chopped anchovy fillets
- Finely chopped shallots or scallions
- Grated lemon zest and juice
- Grated orange zest and juice
- Finely chopped shrimp

Marinades

These are highly flavored liquid mixtures in which the fish can be soaked before grilling. They help to keep it moist while cooking as well as adding flavor. Generally, the longer the fish is marinated, the more flavor it absorbs. It should be turned frequently in the marinade and then drained thoroughly and patted dry with paper towels before grilling. Marinades can be made with the following ingredients:

- Olive, corn, nut, and sesame oils
- Fruit juices
- Plain yogurt
- Ground and whole spices
- Honey, hoisin sauce, and soy sauce
- Minced garlic and finely chopped onion and shallots
- Fresh and dried herbs, especially tarragon, parsley, cilantro, fennel, bay leaves, and sage.

Sauces

A wide range of sauces can be served with grilled fish, many of which can be purchased ready-made.

- Hollandaise sauce adds a lemony, creamy flavor to fish.
- Salsas, flavored with cilantro, tomatoes, chiles, and red onions, make a fresh, spicy addition to many grilled fish dishes and are especially good with shellfish.
- Rouille, a Provençal sauce, is made with red bell peppers, garlic, and chiles (optional). Traditionally it is served with bouillabaisse but it tastes equally good with grilled white and oily fish.
- Tartare sauce, a classic mayonnaise flavored with herbs, capers, and gherkins, complements most grilled white fish.
- Aioli, the great garlic mayonnaise of Provence, goes well with Mediterranean grilled fish dishes.
- Yogurt, flavored with chives, mint, lemon, or cucumber, is wonderful with grilled fish in the Greek or Middle Eastern style. Alternatively, spices can be added to the yogurt to make an Indian-style sauce.

Fish for grilling

There is a wide range of fish and shellfish that are suitable for grilling, including the following:

White fish

You can grill a variety of white fish, whole on the bone or cut into steaks or fillets. Choose from the following:
- Whole flounder, Dover sole, and striped bass, or sea bass
- Fish steaks, e.g. cod, halibut, swordfish
- Fish fillets, e.g. cod, monkfish, halibut, orange roughy

Oily fish

You can grill whole mackerel, herrings, red snapper, or trout. Large oily fish, such as salmon or tuna, can be cut into steaks or fillets, or cooked whole on a grill wrapped in foil.

Shellfish

Lobster, crab, jumbo shrimp, shrimp, and scallops all taste wonderful grilled. For maximum flavor, it is best to grill them in their shells, brushing copiously with marinade or a flavored butter.

Kebobs

Cubes of firm-fleshed white fish, such as monkfish or cod, or oily fish, such as tuna, or shrimp can all be marinated and then threaded on to kebob skewers. Brush frequently with oil or marinate while grilling to prevent them drying out, and turn several times so that the fish cooks evenly. Do not over-cook or the fish will start to disintegrate and fall off the skewers.

Grilling times for fish

Type of fish	Grilling time
Whole Dover sole	4–6 minutes each side
White fish fillets	2–3 minutes each side
Fish steaks, 6 oz each	5–6 minutes each side
Whole fish	5 minutes each side

Choosing fish

The important thing when buying fish is that it should be really fresh. It should smell faintly and pleasantly fishy — avoid fish that smells unpleasantly strong with an ammonia aroma. The scales should be firm, bright, and iridescently shiny and should not cling tightly. The flesh should be elastic to the touch, and the eyes should be clear, bright, and sparkling, not sunken, cloudy, or dull. Look for bright red feathery gills and check that any flesh, if exposed, is clear without a greenish tinge.

Choosing shellfish

Shellfish may be bought live or cooked, in which case it should have a bright, shiny shell with all the legs and claws attached. Mussels are always best bought live to insure safety and freshness. The shells should be undamaged and closed tightly without any cracks. Discard any that are open or have damaged shells.

Cleaning and preparing fish

If you are squeamish about preparing fish don't be afraid to ask the person serving on the fish counter to do this for you. However, cleaning fish yourself is easy and takes very little time.

Cleaning a whole round fish

1 Scrape off the scales by pushing them the wrong way with a sharp knife from the tail end toward the head.

2 Rinse under running cold water and then slit open the fish along its belly from behind the gills to just above the tail. Remove the entrails and rinse the body cavity under running cold water.

3 Cut off any fins, spikes, and gills with a sharp knife or a pair of kitchen scissors. Cut off the head and tail, if wished.

Cleaning a flat fish

1 Wash the fish, pat dry with paper towels, and place it, dark side up, on a flat surface.

2 Make a slit with a sharp knife behind the gills and scrape out the entrails.

3 Wash under running cold water, cut off the fins.

Filleting a round fish

1 If skinning the fish, make a slit in the skin around the head on one side and then loosen the skin.

2 Pull the skin gently but firmly down toward the tail and cut it off. Repeat on the other side.

3 Cut off the head and then carefully cut along the backbone of the fish, working from the head end toward the tail. Gently ease the flesh away from the bone with a thin filleting knife.

4 Open out the fish and cut off the fillet at the tail. Repeat on the other side.

Filleting a flat fish

1 Lay the flat fish, dark skin uppermost, on a flat work surface. Cut off the fins and trim the edges with a sharp knife or scissors.

2 Slice through the dark skin at the tail end of the fish and lift it up slightly to separate it from the flesh. Holding the skin in one hand and keeping the fish flat, gently pull off the skin from tail to head.

3 Insert the knife blade between the white flesh and the slightly pink edge just below the head and cut along the length of the fish.

4 Cut down the center of the backbone, working from head to tail to separate the top two fillets.

5 Make small cuts from the backbone toward the sides and lift the fillets up.

6 Turn the fish over and fillet the other side in the same way.

BARBECUED RED SNAPPER

6 red snapper, cleaned, heads removed
1 lemon, cut into 6 wedges
24 blanched almonds, toasted
1 small onion, finely chopped
6 tablespoons olive oil
2 tablespoons coarsely
chopped parsley
salt and pepper

To serve:
1–2 tablespoons capers
1 cup mayonnaise

1 Make a small slit in each fish and press a wedge of lemon into it, together with 4 almonds. Put the red snapper in a shallow dish. Sprinkle with the chopped onion, olive oil, and parsley, and salt and pepper to taste. Cover the dish and marinate in the refrigerator for at least 6 hours.*

2 Remove the red snapper from the oil and place on the greased grill of a preheated barbecue or under the broiler. If the bars of the barbecue are wide apart, place the fish on a smaller greased grid laid over the barbecue grill or on a double layer of kitchen foil placed, shiny side uppermost, on top of the grill. Cook the fish for about 5 minutes, then carefully turn them over and cook for a further 5–6 minutes, until completely cooked.

3 Stir the capers into the mayonnaise and serve alongside the red snapper.

*The red snapper could be prepared in advance and marinated for up to 8 hours.

Serves 6
Preparation time: 30 minutes, plus 6 hours marinading time
Cooking time: 10–12 minutes

SOY MARINATED ORANGE ROUGHY

Fish responds well to marinades, absorbing the new flavors as its own increases. This marinade is particularly good for a mild-tasting fish, especially if it has been frozen.

**6 medium orange roughy, about
12 ounces each, skin removed
4 tablespoons soy sauce
3 tablespoons dry sherry
4 tablespoons peanut oil
2 tablespoons fresh lime juice
3 scallions, green tops only,
cut into very fine rings
2 garlic cloves, very finely chopped
salt and pepper**

1 Rinse the fish and pat dry with paper towels. Arrange in one layer in a large shallow dish.

2 Mix the soy sauce, sherry, oil, and lime juice together and pour over the fish. Cover and leave at room temperature for 1 hour, turning 2–3 times.*

3 Remove the fish from the marinade and cook under a preheated very hot broiler or over a hot barbecue for 5–7 minutes each side, brushing occasionally with a little marinade.

4 Put the rest of the marinade into a small heavy saucepan and bring to the boil, either on the stove or over the barbecue. Add the scallions and garlic, and boil for 1 minute.

5 Transfer the fish to individual serving plates, spoon over some of the juices, onions, and garlic and serve immediately, sprinkled with a little salt, if wished, and a good grinding of pepper.

*The fish may be marinated for up to 6 hours. Keep it covered and chilled and bring to room temperature before cooking.

Serves 6
Preparation time: 10 minutes, plus 1 hour marinading time
Cooking time: 10–15 minutes

RED SNAPPER
GRILLED WITH WALNUT AND PARSLEY PESTO

The distinctive flavor of red snapper is complemented by a walnut and parsley pesto.

4 x 8-ounce small red snapper, scaled and cleaned, washed and dried, heads removed

Parsley pesto:
½ cup walnut pieces, toasted
4 scallions, chopped
I garlic clove, minced
2 tablespoons chopped parsley
4 tablespoons extra-virgin olive oil
salt and pepper

To garnish:
lemon wedges
parsley sprigs

I First make the parsley pesto. Place the toasted walnuts, scallions, garlic, parsley, and olive oil in a food processor or blender and blend until smooth. Season to taste and transfer to a bowl.

2 Preheat the barbecue or the overhead broiler. Spread the fish inside and out with a little of the pesto. Place the fish on the barbecue or broiler pan and cook for 4–5 minutes on each side, until charred and cooked through.

3 Serve the fish with extra pesto, and garnish with lemon wedges and sprigs of parsley.

Serves 4
Preparation time: 15 minutes
Cooking time: 4–5 minutes

RED SNAPPER GRILLED IN VINE LEAVES

A good way to cook red snapper is to wrap them in vine leaves, which lend a tangy flavor to the fish. You can leave the fish whole or, if you prefer, they can be cleaned before enclosing them in the vine leaves. Packaged in cans or sachets, vine leaves preserved in brine are available in most markets and gourmet food stores. Prepare them for use as follows: put them into a large bowl and cover with boiling water. Allow the water to cool slightly, then gently ease the leaves apart in the water. Leave the leaves for 20 minutes, then drain and transfer to a bowl of cold water. Drain the leaves once again and spread them out to dry, vein sides uppermost. When the leaves are thoroughly dry they are ready for use.

4 small red snapper, scaled and washed
6 tablespoons olive oil
2 bay leaves, crushed
1 tablespoon thyme leaves
1 tablespoon chopped chives
1 teaspoon crushed black peppercorns
½ teaspoon salt
2 garlic cloves, finely chopped
2 tablespoons lemon juice
12 large preserved vine leaves, rinsed well

1 Put the fish in a shallow dish. Mix together the olive oil, herbs, peppercorns, salt, garlic, and lemon juice and pour over the fish.
2 Turn the fish in the flavored oil, cover and leave to marinate in the refrigerator for 2 hours.*
3 Remove the red snapper, reserving the oil, and wrap each one in 3 vine leaves. Fold one over the head, one over the tail, and one around the middle of each fish.
4 Brush the vine leaf wrappings with the reserved flavored oil.
5 Place the fish on the oiled grill of a preheated barbecue or under an overhead broiler and cook for 4 minutes. Turn the fish over carefully and cook for a further 4 minutes on the other side.
6 Serve the fish in their vine leaf wrappings.

*The fish can be prepared in advance, covered and left to marinate in the refrigerator for up to 8 hours in total.

Serves 4
Preparation time: 25 minutes, plus 2 hours marinading time
Cooking time: about 8 minutes

RED SNAPPER
WITH OLIVES, CAPERS, AND OREGANO

If you prefer red snapper with a really crisp skin, fill the cavity of each fish with the oregano, parsley, olives, capers, and garlic, then brush with oil and cook directly over a well-oiled barbecue grill.

6 small red snapper, scaled and cleaned
2 tablespoons chopped oregano
2 tablespoons chopped parsley
½ cup pitted black olives, sliced
2 tablespoons capers
4 tablespoons olive oil
1 garlic clove, minced
salt and pepper

1 Sprinkle the fish inside and out with salt and pepper.

2 Fill the cavity of each fish with half of the chopped oregano and parsley.

3 Place each fish on a rectangle of oiled kitchen foil and pull up the sides.

4 Mix the remaining oregano and parsley with the sliced black olives, capers, olive oil, and garlic. Spoon the mixture evenly over the fish.

5 Cover each fish with a lid of foil, pinching the edges together well to seal.*

6 Cook on the greased grill of a preheated barbecue or under an overhead broiler until the fish are tender—about 20 minutes. Serve with baked potatoes.

*Can be prepared up to 6 hours in advance.

Serves 6
Preparation time: 20 minutes
Cooking time: 20–25 minutes

BARBECUED RED SNAPPER
WITH CORIANDER SEEDS AND GARLIC

6 red snapper, cleaned, heads removed
3 tablespoons olive oil
2 tablespoons coriander seeds,
lightly crushed
3–4 garlic cloves, finely chopped
salt and pepper

To garnish:
lemon slices
bay leaves

1 Rinse the snapper quickly and pat dry. Brush with 1 tablespoon of the oil and leave for 5 minutes.

2 Heat the remaining oil in a skillet, add the coriander seeds and garlic and fry for 2 minutes.

3 Brush the fish with some of this mixture, sprinkle with the salt and pepper, and cook over a preheated hot barbecue (or under a hot broiler) for 4–5 minutes. Turn and brush with the rest of the oil, then grill for 4–5 minutes until crisp. Garnish with sliced lemon and bay leaves and serve immediately.

Serves 6
Preparation time: 5 minutes
Cooking time: 15–20 minutes

GRILLED FISH WITH OREGANO

3 pounds sardines, thawed if frozen
¼ cup olive oil
3–4 tablespoons lemon juice
1 tablespoon dried oregano
1 garlic clove, minced
salt and pepper

To serve:
lemon wedges
thinly sliced brown bread and butter

1 Rinse the fish under running cold water and pat dry. Cover the grill or broiler rack with kitchen foil and arrange the sardines on top. Heat the grill or broiler.

2 Put a good pinch of salt and a generous grinding of black pepper into a bowl. Beat in the olive oil, then the lemon juice, and add the dried oregano and garlic.

3 Brush each fish with a little of the oil mixture, then cook under a hot grill for 3–4 minutes.

4 Turn the fish over and brush with the remaining mixture, then cook for a further 3 minutes, until crisp. Serve at once with the lemon wedges and thinly sliced brown bread and butter.

Serves 4–6
Preparation time: 20–30 minutes
Cooking time: 6–8 minutes

FISH ESCABECHE

In the United States, we are not accustomed to eating fried fish cold, but it is well worth trying, especially when the fish is marinated afterwards, as in this recipe.

20 small sardines
3 tablespoons plain flour
about 1¼ cups olive oil
2 garlic cloves, minced
½ teaspoon powered saffron (optional)
1 teaspoon ground ginger
4 tablespoons lemon juice
1 lemon, thinly sliced
4 small bay leaves
salt and pepper

1 If preferred, clean the sardines, otherwise leave them whole.
2 Wash the fish and pat them dry with paper towels. Dust them evenly with the flour.
3 Using ⅔ cup olive oil, shallow-fry the fish for about 3 minutes on each side, until lightly golden. Remove and drain on paper towels.
4 Put the fish into a shallow serving dish. Mix the remaining olive oil with the garlic, saffron (if using), ginger, salt and pepper to taste, and the lemon juice. Pour over the fish.
5 Lay the lemon slices and bay leaves on top.
6 Cover the fish and marinate in the refrigerator for 24 hours, turning the fish from time to time.* Serve with crusty bread.

*The dish can be prepared in advance but must not be chilled for more than 36 hours.

Serves 4
Preparation time: 20–25 minutes, plus marinading overnight
Cooking time: about 6 minutes

BARBECUED TROUT WITH GARLIC AND ROSEMARY

2 garlic cloves, minced
2 sprigs rosemary, divided
into short lengths
4 trout, about 8 ounces each, cleaned
6 tablespoons olive oil
finely grated zest of ½ lemon
3 tablespoons lemon juice
salt and pepper

To garnish:
16 blanched almonds
16 pitted green olives

1 Mix together the garlic and rosemary and use to fill the body cavity of each trout. Lay the fish in a shallow dish. Mix the olive oil with salt and pepper to taste and the lemon zest and juice. Spoon evenly over the trout.

2 Cover the fish and chill for 3–4 hours.*

3 Remove the trout from the marinade and drain, reserving the marinade. Place the fish on the greased grill of a preheated barbecue and grill for 6 minutes.

4 Brush the trout on both sides with the marinade, then turn over, baste again, and grill on the other side for a further 6 minutes, or until they are tender.

5 Meanwhile, press an almond into each green olive, then roll the olives lightly in the remaining marinade.

6 Arrange the cooked trout on a serving dish, garnish with the halved almond-stuffed olives, lemon slices, fresh rosemary and serve with a green salad.

*Provided the trout are really fresh, they can be marinated for up to 24 hours.

Serves 4
Preparation time: 10 minutes, plus 3–4 hours marinading time
Cooking time: about 12 minutes

GRILLED TROUT WITH GROUND ALMOND PASTE

6 small trout, about 10 ounces each, cleaned but heads and tails left on
1½ cups ground almonds
4–6 tablespoons olive oil
1 tablespoon lemon juice
2 tablespoons finely chopped parsley
salt and pepper
sprigs of chervil, to garnish

1 Rinse the trout quickly in cold water and pat dry with paper towels.

2 Put the ground almonds in a bowl, add 4 tablespoons oil, season well with salt and pepper, and add the lemon juice and parsley. The paste should be thin enough to coat the fish without falling off. If it is too thick, add extra oil.

3 Smear the paste over each fish. Grill over a very hot barbecue (or under a hot broiler) for 7–10 minutes on each side, until the fish is cooked and the skin is beautifully crisp and deep golden. Garnish with chervil sprigs and serve at once.

Serves 6
Preparation time: 15 minutes
Cooking time: 15–20 minutes

GRILLED DOVER SOLE WITH LIME BUTTER

6 Dover soles, about 10–12 ounces each
1½ sticks sweet butter, softened
grated zest of 1 lime
3 tablespoons lime juice
1-inch piece ginger root, peeled
and grated
salt and pepper
finely chopped parsley, to serve

1 To skin the soles, start with the black skin, making a cut with a very sharp knife just above the tail. Slip the knife under the skin and loosen enough to give you a good grip (it sometimes helps to dip your fingers into salt before taking hold of the skin). Holding the tail very firmly in one hand (again salting the fingers first), pull the skin sharply away from the flesh. When you reach the head, merely snip the skin off with sharp scissors, leaving the head intact. Repeat on the other side.

2 Rinse the soles and pat dry, then arrange on a grill rack or broiler pan (if they do not all fit, cook them in two batches, keeping the first batch warm).

3 Mash the butter with all the ingredients except the parsley, then spread about a tablespoon over one side of each fish. Grill, buttered-side up, over a fairly high heat or under the broiler, for 3–5 minutes, depending upon the thickness of the fish (5 minutes per side is enough for a sole 1-inch thick).

4 Turn the fish over, spread the second side with a tablespoon of the butter, and grill until opaque and tender. Transfer to a serving dish and pour the pan juices over the top. Sprinkle with parsley and serve immediately.

Serves 6
Preparation time: 15 minutes
Cooking time: 10 minutes

SARDINES WITH SALSA VERDE

Salsa verde is a green herb sauce that complements the flavor of the sardines perfectly.

4 small sardines, scaled and cleaned, washed and dried
¹/₂ cup parsley leaves
¹/₄ cup fresh mixed herbs, e.g. basil, chives, mint, parsley
I garlic clove, chopped
I tablespoon capers, drained and washed
2 canned anchovy fillets in oil, drained and chopped
I teaspoon Dijon mustard
¹/₂ cup extra-virgin olive oil
salt and pepper
lime wedges, to serve
sprigs of basil, to garnish

1 Preheat the barbecue or a broiler. If using a broiler, place the sardines on an oiled broiler pan.
2 Place all the remaining ingredients in a food processor or blender with 2 tablespoons of warm water, and blend to a smooth paste. Season to taste.
3 Spread a little of the salsa over the fish and grill for 3 minutes. Turn the fish over, spread with a little more salsa and grill for a further 3 minutes, until the sardines are cooked.
4 Serve the sardines immediately with extra salsa verde, lime wedges and sprigs of basil.

Serves 4
Preparation time: 10 minutes
Cooking time: 6 minutes

SEA BASS AND FENNEL BAKED IN FOIL

1 sea bass, about 2 pounds, scaled and cleaned, washed and dried
6 tablespoons olive paste (see below)
1 bulb fennel, sliced very finely
2 thyme sprigs
2 rosemary sprigs
grated zest and juice of 1 lemon
4 tablespoons dry white wine
4 tablespoons olive oil, plus extra for greasing
pepper

1 Grease a large piece of kitchen foil. Season the cavity of the fish with freshly ground pepper, spread with a little of the olive paste and stuff with a couple of slices of fennel and the herbs. Spread the remaining olive paste over the fish.

2 Arrange half of the remaining fennel slices in the center of the greased kitchen foil and lay the fish on top. Scatter the remaining slices of fennel over the fish and carefully gather up the sides and ends of the foil. Pour in the lemon zest and juice, the wine, and oil, then fold the edges of the foil over, sealing in the fish. Wrap a second sheet of foil around the fish with the seam on the opposite side to the first. (This enables you to turn the the fish over halfway through cooking.)

3 Place the fish parcel on the barbecue and cook over medium-hot coals for 25–30 minutes, turning halfway through, until the fish is cooked. Serve straight from the parcel with potatoes and green vegetables or a salad.

Serves 4
Preparation time: 15 minutes
Cooking time: 25–30 minutes

OLIVE PASTE

This delicious purée of olives, anchovies, and capers provides a tasty spread for toast and pizzas, as well as a sauce to accompany grilled fish.

1 cup pitted black olives
2 garlic cloves, chopped
2 tablespoons capers, drained and washed
2 canned anchovy fillets in oil, drained and chopped
1 tablespoon chopped parsley
1 teaspoon chopped thyme
a pinch of mustard powder
2 tablespoons extra-virgin olive oil
pepper

1 Place all the ingredients except the oil in a food processor or blender and blend to a smooth paste. Transfer to a jar, stir in the oil, and seal. Keep in the refrigerator for up to 1 week, and use as required.

Makes approximately ⅔ cup
Preparation time: 5 minutes

GRILLED SEA BASS WITH PARSLEY, LEMON, AND DILL WEED

Although this dish has a better flavor if cooked over a barbecue or an open fire, it can be cooked under an overhead broiler. However, make sure that the fish is far enough away from the heat that it does not char before it is cooked. If cooking on the barbecue, use a fish clamp to hold the fish so that it does not collapse when it is turned over.

1 sea bass, about 2½ pounds, scaled and cleaned
3 tablespoons coarsely chopped parsley
juice and grated zest of 2 lemons
4 tablespoons olive oil
salt and pepper
4 sprigs of dill weed

To garnish:
lemon wedges
small sprigs of dill weed

1 Put the prepared fish into a large oval dish. Mix together the parsley, lemon juice and zest, olive oil, and salt and pepper to taste, and pour over the fish. Cover and chill for 4 hours.*

2 Remove the fish, reserving the marinade for basting. Carefully open up the cavity and insert the sprigs of fresh dill weed.

3 Grease the fish clamp with oil and fit the stuffed fish inside.

4 Lay the clamp over the greased grill of a preheated barbecue and cook for 10–15 minutes.

5 Turn the fish over, brushing it on both sides with some of the marinade.

6 Grill for a further 10 minutes, or until the fish is tender — test with the tip of a knife close to the bone.

7 Arrange the cooked fish on a serving dish and garnish with lemon wedges and dill weed.

*The whole fish could be marinated in the refrigerator for up to 8 hours.

Serves 4-6
Preparation time: 20 minutes, plus 4 hours marinading time
Cooking time: about 25 minutes

MACKEREL WITH DILL STUFFING

4 small mackerel, cleaned
dill stuffing (see below)
olive oil
juice of 1 lemon
parsley sprigs, to garnish

To serve:
lemon wedges
crusty bread

1 Leave the mackerel whole, but with their heads and tails cut off. This leaves a neat pocket to fill with the stuffing. Make the dill stuffing and press it into the cavity in each fish. Make 3 diagonal cuts on each side of the fish, and pour a little olive oil and lemon juice over each one.

2 Grill the stuffed mackerel under fierce heat for 2–3 minutes, then lower the heat for another 5–6 minutes, basting frequently with more oil and lemon juice. Turn over, baste again, and cook the other side for 8 minutes. Garnish with parsley sprigs and serve with plenty of lemon wedges and crusty bread.

Serves 4
Preparation time: 10 minutes
Cooking time: 16 minutes

DILL STUFFING

1 small onion, chopped
¼ stick butter
1 cup fresh bread crumbs
2 tablespoons chopped dill weed
1 egg, beaten
salt and pepper

1 Fry the onion in the butter in a skillet until light brown. Remove from the heat and stir in the bread crumbs. Add salt and pepper to taste, then stir in the chopped dill weed. Stir the beaten egg into the stuffing mixture and use to stuff the fish before grilling.

VARIATION
Follow the recipe for dill stuffing, substituting 3 tablespoons of chopped parsley for the chopped dill. Use to stuff small fish, such as trout and mackerel, before grilling.

GRILLED RED SNAPPER
WITH PESTO AND TOMATO SAUCE

**4 red snapper steaks,
about 6 ounces each
6 tablespoons olive oil
4 large tomatoes, skinned,
seeded, and chopped
4 anchovy fillets, chopped
3 tablespoons pesto
salt and pepper**

1 Season the red snapper steaks on both sides with salt and pepper and brush with 2 tablespoons of the olive oil.

2 Cook on the greased grill of a preheated barbecue for 4–5 minutes on each side, putting the fish on a special grid if the bars of the barbecue are very wide apart.

3 Meanwhile, make the sauce. Heat the remaining olive oil in a pan. Add the tomatoes and anchovy fillets, salt and pepper and cook gently for 5 minutes.

4 Stir the pesto into the tomato and anchovy mixture.

5 Put the red snapper steaks on a serving dish and spoon the sauce over. Serve with green salad and lots of crusty bread.

Serves 4
Preparation time: 4–5 minutes
Cooking time: about 10 minutes

CAJUN-STYLE COD

When making guacamole, be sure to include the flesh near the skin of the avocado
— this is what provides the bright green color.

4 garlic cloves, minced
I teaspoon salt
2 tablespoons chopped oregano
2 tablespoons chopped thyme
I teaspoon whole cumin seeds
I–2 teaspoons chili powder
4 green cardamom pods, seeds removed
12 whole allspice berries
2 teaspoons whole mixed peppercorns
2 teaspoons paprika
2 tablespoons all-purpose flour
I stick butter, melted
4 cod fillets, about 7–8 ounces each
2 ripe plantains
juice of ½ lime
lime wedges, to garnish

Guacamole:
I large ripe avocado
juice of I lime
I large tomato, skinned,
seeded, and chopped
I tablespoon chopped cilantro
I small onion, finely chopped
salt and pepper

1 To make the guacamole, first cut the avocado in half and remove the seed. Scoop out the flesh into a blender or food processor, add the lime juice and blend until smooth. Spoon the avocado mixture into a bowl and stir in the chopped tomato, cilantro, and onion. Add salt and pepper to taste. Cover the surface with plastic wrap and set aside.

2 To make the spiced flour, place the garlic, salt, and all the herbs and spices in a mortar. Grind with a pestle until smooth. Alternatively, use a coffee grinder kept specifically for grinding spices. Tip the mixture into a shallow dish and stir in the flour.

3 Pour the melted butter into another shallow dish. Dip the fish fillets into the melted butter, then dust with the spiced flour mixture. Place on an oiled barbecue grill over moderately hot coals. Cook for 2–3 minutes, turn over and then cook the other side for 2–3 minutes.

4 Meanwhile, cut the unpeeled plantains in half lengthwise, and brush with the lime juice. Place on the grill, skin-side down. Cook for 2 minutes, until the skin is well blackened, then turn over and grill for 1 minute, or until the flesh is just cooked.

5 Serve the Cajun fish with the guacamole, grilled plantains, and lime wedges. Add a crisp green salad if liked.

Serves 4

Preparation time: 25 minutes
Cooking time: 4–6 minutes

GRILLED FISH STEAKS WITH MINT PESTO

4 halibut or cod steaks,
about 6 ounces each
olive oil for basting
lemon juice
lemon slices, to garnish (optional)
salt and pepper

Mint pesto:
6 tablespoons chopped mint
1 tablespoon chopped parsley
1 garlic clove, chopped
1 tablespoon freshly grated
Parmesan cheese
1 tablespoon heavy cream
1 teaspoon balsamic vinegar
3 tablespoons extra-virgin olive oil

1 Place the halibut or cod on a grill or broiler pan, brush with olive oil and squeeze over a little lemon juice. Season with salt and pepper and cook the fish over a preheated hot barbecue (or under a hot broiler) for 3–4 minutes on each side, until golden and cooked through.

2 Meanwhile, place all the ingredients for the pesto in a food processor or blender and blend until fairly smooth; season to taste and transfer to a bowl.

3 Serve the fish steaks spread with a spoonful of the pesto and accompanied by steamed green vegetables. Garnish with lemon slices, if wished and serve with roast potatoes and steamed green vegetables.

Serves 4
Preparation time: 10 minutes
Cooking time: 6–8 minutes

FISH STEAKS WITH BLACK BEANS AND GINGER

4 thick halibut or cod steaks,
about 6 ounces each
1 red chile, seeded and finely chopped
1½ tablespoons fermented
black beans, finely chopped
1-inch piece fresh ginger root,
peeled and finely chopped
finely grated zest and juice of 1 lime
1–2 tablespoons light soy sauce
2 garlic cloves, minced
2 tablespoons Shaosing rice
wine or dry sherry
2 teaspoons sesame oil
2 scallions, finely sliced
pepper

1 Place the fish in a single layer in a shallow dish. Mix the remaining ingredients in a bowl. Pour the mixture over the fish, turning to coat. Cover and marinate for 30 minutes.

2 Place each fish steak on a square of kitchen foil. Turn up the edges of the foil slightly. Divide the marinade between the squares, then gather up the edges of the kitchen foil and press them together to seal.

3 Cook the foil parcels on the barbecue grill over hot coals for 10–15 minutes. Serve at once, in the foil parcels, with plain rice or egg noodles, and steamed vegetables. Diners open their own parcels and mix the fragrant juices with the rice or egg noodles.

Serves 4
Preparation time: 15 minutes, plus 30 minutes marinading time
Cooking time: 10–15 minutes

BARBECUED FISH STEAKS WITH GARLIC BUTTER

A simple supper dish that is transformed as soon as the garlic butter is spooned on top.

**4 x 6-ounce fish steaks, e.g. halibut,
swordfish, salmon, washed and dried
orange and lemon wedges, to garnish
(optional)**

Marinade:
**4 tablespoons olive oil, plus
extra for greasing
grated zest of I orange
grated zest of I lemon
I garlic clove, minced
I fresh red or green chile,
seeded and sliced
4 thyme sprigs
2 bay leaves, bruised
2 teaspoons coriander seeds, crushed**

Garlic butter:
**I stick sweet butter
2 shallots or small onions, diced
I garlic clove, minced
2 tablespoons chopped fresh herbs
salt and pepper**

1 Place the fish steaks in a shallow ceramic or plastic dish. Combine all the marinade ingredients, pour over the fish, cover, and marinate for several hours, or preferably overnight.

2 Remove the fish from the refrigerator and allow to return to room temperature for 1 hour.

3 To make the garlic butter. Melt 1 tablespoon of the butter and fry the shallots and garlic for about 5 minutes, or until softened but not colored. Allow the mixture to cool, then beat into the remaining butter with the herbs and seasoning.

4 Remove the fish from the marinade and place on an oiled barbecue grid. Brush with the marinade juices and cook for 3–4 minutes on each side, basting frequently, until the fish is charred and cooked through. Serve at once, topped with the garlic butter and garnished with lemon and orange wedges, if wished.

Serves 4
Preparation time: 15 minutes, plus marinading overnight
Cooking time: 11–13 minutes

GRILLED SALMON FILLETS WITH PESTO AND LEMON BUTTER RICE

Grilling fish is quick and simple, and the addition of pesto or another herb paste elevates it
into something special. The lemon butter rice complements the fish perfectly.

¾ cup long-grain rice
grated zest and juice of 1 lemon
4 x 5-ounce salmon fillets,
washed and dried
olive oil to baste
½ stick butter
basil leaves, to garnish (optional)

Pesto:
1 garlic clove, chopped
handful of basil leaves
2 tablespoons pine nuts
3 tablespoons extra-virgin olive oil
1 tablespoon freshly grated
Parmesan cheese
salt and pepper

1 Bring a large saucepan of water to to a rolling boil, add the rice and lemon zest, return to the boil and simmer for 10–12 minutes, until the rice is cooked.

2 Meanwhile, make the pesto. Put all the ingredients in a food processor or blender and blend until smooth. Season to taste, then set the mixture aside.

3 Pull out any bones that may remain in the salmon and place the fillets on a preheated oiled barbecue or broiler pan, skin-side down. Brush with oil and grill for 3 minutes. Turn the salmon over and grill for a further 2–3 minutes, until cooked.

4 Drain the rice and immediately stir in the lemon juice and butter. Season to taste. Serve the salmon fillets on a bed of rice with the pesto. Garnish with basil leaves, if wished.

Serves 4
Preparation time: 10 minutes
Cooking time: 20 minutes

SALMON STEAKS WITH ORANGE SAUCE

2 tablespoons orange juice
4 salmon steaks, about 4 ounces each
vegetable oil, for brushing
¼ stick butter, melted
orange wedges, to garnish

Orange sauce:
I large egg
pinch of mustard powder
2 teaspoons grated orange zest
I tablespoon orange juice
½ cup corn oil
salt and pepper
orange shreds, to garnish

I Sprinkle the orange juice over the salmon steaks, season with pepper, and set aside at room temperature for at least 15 minutes.
2 Brush a grill rack with oil. Brush the salmon steaks with half of the melted butter and grill for 4 minutes over a preheated hot barbecue or under a hot broiler. Turn the steaks over, brush them with the remaining butter and grill for 5 minutes.
3 To make the sauce, put all the ingredients except the oil in a blender. Blend for 2–3 seconds. Then, with the machine running, pour in the oil gradually. Taste the sauce and adjust the seasoning if necessary, and garnish with shreds of orange.
Serve with asparagus and orange wedges.

Serves 4
Preparation time: 10 minutes, plus 15 minutes marinading time
Cooking time: 10 minutes

TERIYAKI BARBECUED SALMON STEAKS

The mixture used to glaze these salmon steaks is a sweet and sour Chinese-style sauce. There are several varieties of Teriyaki marinade sauce available but a thinner sauce is probably preferable to a thicker one.

I tablespoon corn oil,
plus extra for greasing
I tablespoon sesame oil
6 tablespoons teriyaki marinade sauce
2 tablespoons rice or white wine vinegar
I tablespoon lime juice
2 tablespoons clear honey
4 x 6-ounce salmon steaks,
washed and dried

I Place all the ingredients except the salmon steaks in a small saucepan and bring to the boil. Simmer rapidly for 10 minutes, or until reduced to a thick, glossy sauce. Set aside to cool.
2 Brush a preheated barbecue grid with oil. Brush the salmon steaks all over with the glaze and cook for 3–4 minutes on each side, until slightly charred and cooked through. Serve immediately with any remaining glaze.

Serves 4
Preparation time: 5 minutes
Cooking time: 16–18 minutes

GRILLED MACKEREL JAPANESE-STYLE

4 x 6-ounce mackerel fillets
(with skin on)
1 cup finely grated mooli
(white radish)
2 tablespoons soy sauce
salt
lemon wedges, to garnish

1 Cut the fillets of mackerel in half crosswise and sprinkle lightly with salt. Leave for 5 minutes, then rinse in cold water and pat dry with paper towels. Sprinkle very lightly once again with salt on both sides.

2 Cut a shallow cross in the skin of each fillet to prevent it from curling during cooking. Do not cut deeper than the skin. Grill over a moderate heat for about 5 minutes on each side, until golden. Arrange the fish on 4 serving plates, skin-side uppermost.

3 Lightly squeeze out all the moisture from the grated mooli and divide between the 4 plates. Sprinkle the soy sauce over the mooli and garnish with lemon wedges.

Serves 4
Preparation time: 10 minutes, plus 5 minutes standing time
Cooking time: 10 minutes

TANDOORI FISH

If you use homemade yogurt it is best to stabilize it before heating it, at stage 3.
Stir 2 teaspoons flour into it to make a paste, then heat through slowly, stirring constantly.

1½ pounds haddock or cod fillets, skinned
lemon wedges, to garnish

Sauce:
1¼ cups plain yogurt
2 tablespoons lemon juice
1 small onion, finely chopped
1 tablespoon sweet paprika
½ teaspoon cayenne
1 teaspoon ground cumin
1 tablespoon tomato paste
1 bay leaf
salt and pepper

1 Mix together all the sauce ingredients.

2 Place the fish in a shallow dish. Pour over half of the sauce, cover and leave in the refrigerator to marinate for at least 2 hours. Refrigerate the reserved sauce.

3 Line a broiler with kitchen foil. Remove the fish from the marinade and cook for 6 minutes on each side under a hot broiler. Heat the reserved sauce through gently in a small saucepan.

4 Garnish the fish with lemon wedges and serve the sauce separately. Serve with rice.

Serves 4
Preparation time: 10 minutes, plus 2 hours marinading time
Cooking time: 15 minutes

SWORDFISH STEAKS WITH CHARMOULA AND GRILLED BELL PEPPER SALSA

Swordfish is a firm-fleshed fish which is very suitable for barbecuing. Charmoula is an Arabian sauce which tastes equally delicious with tuna. A non-reactive dish is ceramic or plastic (not metal).

4 swordfish steaks, about 6 ounces each
oil for greasing
1 quantity grilled bell pepper salsa, to serve (see below)
lime wedges, to garnish

Charmoula:
1 teaspoon paprika
¹/₂ teaspoon ground turmeric
¹/₂ teaspoon ground cumin
2 garlic cloves, minced
2 tablespoons chopped fresh cilantro
1 tablespoon lime juice
3 tablespoons extra-virgin olive oil
salt and pepper

1 Place the swordfish in a non-reactive dish. Combine all the charmoula ingredients together and brush over both sides of the fish steaks. Cover and marinate for at least 4 hours, preferably overnight.

2 Brush the preheated barbecue grid with oil and add the swordfish steaks, pouring off any marinade juices into a bowl. Cook the fish for 3–4 minutes on each side, basting with the marinade, until the fish is charred and tender.

3 Serve at once with a spoonful of grilled bell pepper salsa, and garnish with lime wedges, if wished.

Serves 4

Preparation time: 5 minutes, plus 4 hours marinading time
Cooking time: 6–8 minutes

GRILLED BELL PEPPER SALSA

1 large red bell pepper
¹/₂ tablespoon balsamic vinegar
a pinch of sugar
1 tablespoon extra-virgin olive oil, plus extra for brushing
salt and pepper

1 Grill the bell pepper under a preheated hot broiler, turning occasionally, until slightly charred and blistered all over. Put the pepper into a plastic bag for a few minutes, then remove and skin. Seed the pepper over a bowl to catch the juices.

2 Roughly chop the flesh, place in a food processor or blender with the juices, vinegar, and sugar, and blend until smooth. Transfer to a bowl and whisk in the oil, season to taste, then cover and set aside while the fish is cooking.

Serves 4

Preparation time: 10 minutes

BARBECUED MAHIMAHI

1½ pounds mahimahi, tuna, or swordfish
steak, ¾–1 inch thick, cut in 4 equal pieces
4 tablespoons olive oil
2 tablespoons orange juice
1 tablespoon lemon juice
salt and pepper
orange slices, to garnish

Lime butter:
½ stick butter, at room temperature
1 tablespoon lime juice
½ teaspoon grated lime zest

1 Arrange the pieces of fish in a shallow dish in one layer. Mix together the oil, juices, and salt and pepper, then pour over the fish. Cover and marinade in the refrigerator for at least 1 hour, turning the fish over occasionally.
2 Meanwhile, make the lime butter. Put the butter, lime juice, and zest in a food processor or blender and process until well blended. Spoon onto a sheet of kitchen foil and shape into a roll. Wrap in the foil and refrigerate until firm.
3 Remove the fish from the marinade, drain well and grill about 6 inches above hot coals for 3–4 minutes each side, turning once or twice, until firm and opaque outside but still moist in the center.
4 Top each piece of fish with a slice of lime butter and garnish with orange slices. Serve immediately.

Serves 4
Preparation time: 15 minutes, plus 1 hour marinading time
Cooking time: 6–8 minutes

GRILLED SHARK STEAKS

4 shark steaks, about 6 ounces each
1 tablespoon oil
lemon wedges, to garnish

Marinade:
6 tablespoons white wine
2 tablespoons olive oil
4 tablespoons chopped onion or scallions
few drops of Tabasco sauce (optional)
salt and pepper

1 Place the fish in a dish and add the marinade ingredients. Turn the fish over in the marinade so that it absorbs the mixture, and leave for at least 30 minutes, preferably longer.
2 Lift the steaks from the marinade, drain and brush with a little oil. Reserve the marinade. Place the fish steaks on some kitchen foil over a preheated grill (or under a broiler) and cook for 5–6 minutes. Turn over, brush again with oil and continue cooking for the same time on the second side, or until quite tender. Serve immediately, garnished with the lemon wedges.
3 Any leftover marinade can be heated and spooned over the fish just before serving.

Serves 4
Preparation time: 10 minutes, plus 30 minutes marinading time
Cooking time: 10–12 minutes

FILLETS OF SOLE EN PAPILLOTE
WITH TARRAGON, WINE, AND BUTTER

12 large sole fillets, about 2½ pounds
total weight
⅔ cup sweet butter, cut into 6 pieces
6 sprigs fresh tarragon
⅔ cup dry white wine
1 tablespoon olive oil
3–4 tablespoons day-old bread crumbs
salt and pepper

1 If you wish, slice the sole fillets into long thin strips.
2 Cut 6 pieces of kitchen foil into 8-inch squares. Use the pieces of butter to grease each one, then divide the sole between the squares. Dot with the remaining pieces of butter, put a sprig of tarragon on each one, then sprinkle with the wine.
3 Heat the oil in a skillet, add the bread crumbs and stir-fry for 1–2 minutes, adding more oil if necessary, until the crumbs are crisp. Scatter over the sole, season with salt and pepper, and seal the parcels tightly.
4 Cook the parcels over a preheated very hot barbecue for 8–10 minutes, then serve at once in the foil. Plenty of French bread and a chilled dry white wine are the only accompaniments needed.

Serves 6
Preparation time: 10 minutes
Cooking time: 10–12 minutes

ROLLED SKEWERED SOLE FILLETS
WITH TOMATOES AND MOZZARELLA

3 large sole, filleted into quarter fillets
and skinned, washed and dried
4 tablespoons anchovy butter, softened
(see opposite page)
12 sun-dried tomatoes in oil, drained
4 ounces mozzarella cheese,
cut into 12 cubes
olive oil for greasing

1 Spread the underside of each fish fillet with a little anchovy butter. Place 1 sun-dried tomato and a cube of mozzarella at the narrow end of each fillet. Roll up tightly to enclose the filling and thread 3 rolled fillets on to each skewer. Spread the remaining anchovy butter all over the rolled fish.
2 Preheat the broiler. Place the skewers on a broiler pan, lined with greased kitchen foil, and cook for 8–10 minutes, turning frequently, until the fish is cooked and the cheese has melted. Serve immediately with a crisp green salad.

Serves 4
Preparation time: 15 minutes
Cooking time: 8–10 minutes

MARINATED MONKFISH GRILLED WITH HERBS

about 3 pounds monkfish tail
¼ cup olive oil
2 tablespoons lemon juice
2–3 garlic cloves, finely chopped
2 sprigs thyme, leaves stripped from the stems
4 tablespoons finely chopped fresh chives
4 tablespoons finely chopped fresh mint
2 tablespoons cognac
salt and pepper
mint leaves, to garnish

1 Fillet the monkfish into 2 long triangular pieces and place in a shallow dish. Pour over the oil, lemon juice, and garlic and leave, covered but not chilled, for 1 hour.*

2 Mix the herbs with a good pinch of salt and lots of pepper, then remove the fish from its marinade and sprinkle half the herb mixture over one side of each fillet.

3 Brush the grid of the barbecue or broiler pan with oil. Put the monkfish fillets on the grid, sprinkle with half of the cognac and cook over hot coals or under a very hot overhead broiler for 2½–4 minutes, depending on the thickness of the fish and how well done you like it.

4 Turn the fillets over, brush with a little oil, then spread the remaining herbs over the fish and sprinkle over the rest of the cognac. Cook for another 2½–4 minutes, then garnish and serve.

*This dish may be prepared up to 8 hours ahead, covered, and chilled. Bring to room temperature before cooking.

Serves 6
Preparation time: 10 minutes, plus 1 hour marinading time
Cooking time: 5–8 minutes

ANCHOVY BUTTER

This tasty butter, flavored with chopped anchovies, is delicious on grilled fish, or as a pizza topping, or stirred into freshly cooked pasta.

1 stick sweet butter, softened
4 canned anchovy fillets in oil, drained and coarsely chopped
squeeze of lemon juice
pepper

1 Place all the ingredients in a food processor or blender and blend until smooth. Transfer to a bowl, cover, and store for up to 1 week in the refrigerator. Alternatively, roll the butter into a long cylindrical shape, wrap in plastic wrap and freeze for up to 1 month.

Makes 4 ounces
Preparation time: 10 minutes

SALMON KEBOBS WITH VERMOUTH

Tail pieces of salmon are ideal for this recipe but you could also use any firm white fish.

2-pound tailpiece of fresh salmon, skinned
1½ sticks sweet butter, softened
5 tablespoons dry vermouth
1 cup white bread crumbs
1 tablespoon olive oil
2 tablespoons sesame seeds
salt and pepper

To garnish:
lime slices
½ head frisée lettuce

1 Remove the center bone from the salmon, then cut the flesh into 1-inch cubes.

2 Beat the butter with the vermouth, a little salt, and lots of black pepper, beating to make a smooth paste.

3 Put the bread crumbs on a flat plate or work surface, and press the fish lightly into them to coat it all over. Thread on to skewers.

4 If cooking under the broiler, place the skewers in the broiler pan and cook under a preheated, very hot broiler for 5–7 minutes, turning every minute, until the fish is just done. Alternatively, cook over hot coals on the barbecue. Transfer the skewers to individual serving plates and keep warm.

5 Pour any cooking juices from the broiler pan into a small saucepan, add the oil and heat. Stir in the sesame seeds, cook for 1 minute until golden, then pour over the kebobs. Serve immediately garnished with lime slices and frisée lettuce.

Serves 4–6
Preparation time: 25 minutes
Cooking time: 5–7 minutes

OYSTERS WITH SMOKED SALMON

12 oysters
3 ounces smoked salmon, finely chopped
1³/₄ cups canned artichoke hearts, drained and finely chopped
¹/₄ cup grated Swiss cheese
2 tablespoons dried bread crumbs
pepper
lime wedges, to garnish

Herb butter:
³/₄ stick butter, softened
1 tablespoon chopped chervil
1 tablespoon chopped tarragon
2 teaspoons lemon juice

1 First make the herb butter by beating all the ingredients together in a small bowl.
2 Open the oysters. Return the oysters to the deeper rounded shell.
3 Place a little chopped smoked salmon and artichoke on each oyster and dot with the herb butter. Sprinkle with the cheese, bread crumbs, and pepper to taste.
4 Place on a cookie sheet, balancing the oyster shells with kitchen foil if necessary, and cook under a preheated moderate broiler for 10–15 minutes, until golden.
5 Transfer to a warmed serving dish, garnish with lime wedges and serve with brown bread and butter.

Serves 2–4
Preparation time: 15 minutes
Cooking time: 15 minutes

BROILED CRAB

4 small cooked crabs
juice of ¹/₂ lemon
¹/₄ stick butter
1 small onion, finely chopped
¹/₂ cup dry sherry
1 teaspoon Worcestershire sauce
1 teaspoon French mustard
1 teaspoon crumbled thyme
2 teaspoons chopped parsley
1¹/₄ cups heavy cream
2 tablespoons fresh bread crumbs
1 tablespoon grated Parmesan cheese
salt and pepper
4 shrimp, to garnish

1 Twist off the claws and legs from the crabs, then crack open and extract all the meat. Remove the white and brown meat from the body shells. Discard the gray sac and feathered gills.
2 Flake the crab meat into a basin and add the lemon juice. Scrub the shells and set aside.
3 Melt the butter in a pan, add the onion and cook until golden. Pour in the sherry and cook rapidly until reduced by two-thirds.
4 Stir in the Worcestershire sauce, mustard, and herbs. Pour in the cream and cook until thickened, then stir in the crab meat. Season with salt and pepper to taste.
5 Spoon into the crab shells and sprinkle with the bread crumbs and Parmesan cheese. Cook under a preheated moderate broiler until bubbling and golden brown. Serve hot.

Serves 4
Preparation time: 20 minutes
Cooking time: 15 minutes

BARBECUED LOBSTER

2 fresh lobsters, about I pound
each, halved
I small onion, finely chopped
I garlic clove, minced
⅔ cup dry white wine
2 tablespoons tomato paste
4 tablespoons olive oil
½ teaspoon chili powder
I tablespoon chopped fresh oregano
or I teaspoon dried oregano
salt and pepper

I Crack the claws of each lobster half gently with lobster crackers to ensure that they cook evenly on the barbecue.

2 Put the halved lobsters, shell-side downward, in a shallow dish. Mix all the other ingredients together and spoon evenly over the lobster halves. Cover and chill for 1 hour.

3 Drain off any excess marinade from each lobster half and place them, shell-side downward, on the greased grill of a preheated barbecue. Cook for about 15–20 minutes.

4 Turn the lobsters over, brush the flesh with any remaining marinade, and cook for a further 3 minutes. Serve hot with a green salad.

Serves 4
Preparation time: 15–20 minutes, plus 1 hour marinading time
Cooking time: 20–25 minutes

SCALLOP AND SHRIMP BROCHETTES

⅔ cup dry white wine
I tablespoon raspberry vinegar
I tablespoon chopped dill weed
½ teaspoon salt
12 large scallops
1½–2 cucumbers, peeled and cut
into ½-inch slices
8 jumbo shrimp
I tablespoon melted butter
basil leaves, to garnish

I Place the wine, vinegar, dill weed, and salt in a large pan, bring to simmering point and add the scallops and cucumber. Simmer for 1–2 minutes, then remove with a slotted spoon. Reserve the cooking liquid.

2 Place a shrimp at one end of each of 4 long kebob skewers. Arrange the scallops and cucumber alternately on the skewers, then add another shrimp.

3 Brush with the melted butter and cook under a preheated high broiler, or on a barbecue, for about 3 minutes on each side, basting frequently with the reserved cooking liquid.

4 Arrange the brochettes on a warmed serving dish and garnish with basil leaves.

Serves 4
Preparation time: 15 minutes
Cooking time: 6–8 minutes

SPICY BUTTERFLIED SHRIMP

2 pounds uncooked jumbo shrimp
4 tablespoons orange juice
3 tablespoons lime juice
6 tablespoons olive oil
I tablespoon white rum
I garlic clove, minced
I tablespoon dried green
peppercorns, crushed
I–2 dried small hot red chiles, crushed
salt

To garnish:
sprigs of dill weed
lemon wedges

I Remove the shells and tails from the shrimp, then slit each one down the back, part way through so that it will open up and lie flat. Rinse to remove the dark vein, then pat dry.
2 Combine the remaining ingredients, with salt to taste, in a mixing bowl. Add the shrimp and mix into the marinade. Cover and marinate in the refrigerator for at least 4 hours.
3 Thread the shrimp on to skewers, inserting the point of the skewer at the tail end and pushing it through the shrimp to come out at the head end. Reserve the marinade.
4 Grill the shrimp on a barbecue over hot coals for 6–10 minutes, turning and basting occasionally with the reserved marinade. Do not overcook; the shrimp are ready when they change from translucent to opaque pink. Serve hot garnished with sprigs of dill weed and lime wedges.

Serves 4–6
Preparation time: 15 minutes, plus 4 hours marinading time
Cooking time: 6–10 minutes

GRILLED SHRIMPS WITH BASIL BUTTER

24 large uncooked jumbo shrimp,
peeled and heads removed
oil, for greasing
1½ sticks butter
24 large fresh basil leaves,
coarsely chopped
2 large garlic cloves, minced
salt and pepper
I–2 sprigs basil, to garnish

I Put the shrimp on to the greased grill of a preheated barbecue, shell-side downward, and cook for 2 minutes. Turn the shrimp over and cook for a further 2 minutes.
2 Meanwhile, melt the butter in a small pan and add the chopped basil and garlic — this can be done on the side of the barbecue.
3 Arrange the grilled shrimp, flesh-side uppermost, on a bed of salad in a large flat serving dish. Spoon the hot basil butter over the top and garnish with the sprigs of fresh basil.
4 Serve immediately with a simple green salad and lots of warm crusty bread to mop up the basil butter.

Serves 4
Preparation time: 25 minutes
Cooking time: 4–5 minutes

BROILED MUSSELS

4 pounds fresh mussels
1 cup white wine
½ red bell pepper, seeded and chopped
2 garlic cloves, minced
4 tablespoons finely chopped parsley
1½ cups canned tomatoes, drained and chopped
5 tablespoons fresh white bread crumbs
2 tablespoons olive oil
1 tablespoon grated Parmesan cheese
salt and pepper

1 Put the mussels in a large bowl, cover with cold water and discard any that are open or cracked or rise to the surface. Scrub them well under running cold water, removing the beards. Put the cleaned mussels in a large saucepan with the wine and bring to the boil, covered with a closely-fitting lid.

2 Cook the mussels over a medium heat for a few minutes, still covered, and shaking the pan occasionally until they open. Discard any mussels that do not open. Remove the open mussels from the pan and take off and throw away the top half of each shell.

3 In a bowl, mix together the chopped red bell pepper, garlic, parsley, chopped tomatoes, and 4 tablespoons of the bread crumbs. Stir in 1 tablespoon of olive oil and then season to taste with a little salt and pepper.

4 Add a little of this mixture to each of the mussels in their shells and place them in an ovenproof dish. Sprinkle with grated Parmesan cheese and the remaining breadcrumbs and olive oil and bake in a preheated oven at 450°F for 10 minutes. Preheat the broiler and flash the mussels under the hot broiler for a crisp finish.

Serves 4–6
Preparation time: 30 minutes
Cooking time: 10 minutes

GRILLED BUTTERFLIED SHRIMP WITH ROMESCO SAUCE

Nora peppers are sold by some specialist food stores, but if unavailable use 1 large red bell pepper, char-grilled, skinned, and seeded, and 1–2 small dried red chiles, soaked for 20 minutes in cold water and drained.

**12–16 uncooked jumbo shrimp
in their shells
3 tablespoons olive oil
1/2 garlic clove, minced
1 1/2 tablespoons lime juice
salt and pepper
lemon wedges, to serve**

**Sauce:
2 nora peppers, seeded, soaked for
20 minutes in cold water, and drained
4 plump garlic cloves, grilled and skinned
1 cup mixed hazelnuts and blanched
almonds, toasted
small handful of parsley
4 tablespoons red wine vinegar
2/3 cup olive oil
salt and pepper**

1 To make the sauce, pound the peppers, garlic, nuts, parsley, and salt and pepper to a paste in a mortar, or mix in a food processor or blender. Mix in the vinegar, then slowly pour in the oil; the mixture should be thick and almost smooth. Adjust the seasoning and add a little more vinegar if necessary. Transfer to a bowl, cover, and refrigerate for at least 1 day, or up to 1 week; transfer to room temperature 2 hours before serving.

2 Remove the heads and legs from the shrimp. Using sharp scissors, cut each shrimp lengthwise from the head end almost to the tail, leaving the tail intact. Place in a shallow dish. Mix together the remaining ingredients, pour over the shrimp, turn to coat with the marinade, cover and leave for 30 minutes.

3 Cook under a preheated broiler, brushing occasionally with any remaining marinade, until the shrimp have opened out (butterflied) and are bright pink, this should take about 3 minutes. Just before the shrimp are ready, stir the sauce, then serve with the shrimp, accompanied by lemon wedges.

Serves 4

Preparation time: 30 minutes, plus 30 minutes marinading time
Cooking time: 3 minutes

VARIATION

Omit the parsley, reduce the almonds to 1/4 cup, or use 1/4 cup browned hazelnuts and add 8 ounces extra large tomatoes, charred, skinned, and seeded.

LIME FISH KEBOBS WITH PEANUT SAUCE

1½ pounds monkfish fillet, washed, dried,
and cut into large cubes

Marinade:
grated zest and juice of 2 limes
2 garlic cloves, sliced
2 stalks lemon grass, coarsely crushed
1 fresh red chile, seeded and sliced
1 teaspoon grated fresh ginger root
1 tablespoon dark soy sauce
1 tablespoon clear honey
1 tablespoon corn oil

Peanut sauce:
4 tablespoons chopped peanuts
¼ teaspoon crushed chile flakes
1 garlic clove, minced
1 tablespoon dark soy sauce
1 tablespoon lime juice
1 teaspoon clear honey
2 tablespoons double cream
2 tablespoons creamed coconut

To garnish:
lime wedges
chopped cilantro and cilantro sprigs

1 Place the monkfish pieces in a shallow, non-reactive (ceramic or plastic) dish. Blend all the marinade ingredients together and pour over the fish. Cover and marinate overnight.
2 Remove the fish from the refrigerator and allow to return to room temperature for 1 hour.
3 Meanwhile, prepare the peanut sauce. Dry-fry the peanuts in a small saucepan until golden, then add all the remaining ingredients with 6 tablespoons of water. Heat gently until the coconut has melted and bring to the boil, then remove from the heat. Set aside.
4 Strain the marinade juices into a small bowl. Thread the fish cubes on to the skewers and cook on an oiled grid over a hot barbecue for 6–8 minutes, turning and basting frequently with the marinade juices, until the fish is charred and cooked through. Serve at once, garnished with lime wedges and cilantro along with the peanut sauce to dip.

Serves 4
Preparation time: 15 minutes, plus marinading time overnight
Cooking time: 6–8 minutes

BARBECUED SQUID AND SHRIMP

When barbecued, the flavors of the squid and the fresh shrimp can be fully appreciated—this cooking method gives a smoky, sweet, char-grilled taste, a perfect complement to the hot peppery sauce.

12 ounces prepared squid
12 uncooked jumbo shrimp, in their shells

Red bell pepper sauce:
2 red bell peppers
2 fresh chiles
1 tablespoon sherry vinegar
salt and pepper

Marinade:
3 tablespoons chopped fresh oregano
5 tablespoons olive oil
2 shallots or small onions, finely chopped
1 tablespoon lemon juice

1 To prepare the sauce, place the bell peppers and chiles under a hot preheated broiler. Cook the bell peppers for 10–15 minutes and the chiles for 5–6 minutes, turning occasionally.

2 When their skins are charred and well blistered, transfer the chiles and bell peppers to a plastic bag, close the top lightly and set aside to cool.

3 Rub off the charred skin, then cut the bell peppers and chiles in half and discard the seeds. Pat the vegetables dry with paper towels, then place them in a food processor or blender. Add the sherry vinegar and blend until smooth. Season with salt and pepper to taste.

4 Cut the squid flesh into 1-inch squares, then score the squares in a crisscross pattern.

5 Place the squid and shrimp in a shallow dish. Mix the marinade ingredients together and pour over the seafood. Toss to coat, then cover and marinate for about 30–40 minutes.

6 Using a slotted spoon, remove the seafood from the marinade, then pour the marinade into a small picher. Thread the squid and shrimp alternately on to wood or metal skewers.

7 Cook the brochettes on an oiled barbecue grill over moderately hot coals for 6–8 minutes, turning once and basting frequently with the remaining marinade. Place the brochettes in deep soup bowls and pour the sauce over them.

Serves 4
Preparation time: 20 minutes, plus 30–40 minutes marinading time
Cooking time: 6–8 minutes

SHRIMP, SCALLOP, AND PARMA HAM KEBOBS

A classic combination of scallops with Parma ham is glazed with sun-dried tomato paste as it cooks—sun-dried tomato paste is available commercially or you can simply purée a few sun-dried tomatoes with some of the oil from the jar. You will need 4 skewers; if they are wooden, soak them for 30 minutes before use.
A non-reactive dish is plastic or ceramic (not metal).

12 large fresh scallops, cleaned, washed and dried

4 thick slices of Parma ham, cut lengthwise into 3 strips

12 uncooked jumbo shrimp, washed and dried

Marinade:
½ cup extra-virgin olive oil, plus extra for brushing
2 garlic cloves, minced
grated zest of 1 lemon
1 teaspoon ground coriander
1 teaspoon paprika
¼ teaspoon chili powder
2 tablespoons sun-dried tomato paste
lemon wedges, to serve
mango salsa (see below), to serve

1 Prepare the scallops. Wrap each strip of ham around a scallop. Thread 3 shrimp and 3 scallops alternately on to 4 skewers and place in a non-reactive dish.

2 Combine all the marinade ingredients, except the tomato paste, and pour into the dish. Cover and marinate the kebobs for at least 1 hour, or longer if possible.

3 Remove the kebobs from the marinade. Beat the tomato paste into the marinade, then brush over the shrimp and scallops. Brush the barbecue grid with a little oil to prevent the kebobs sticking and cook them for 6–8 minutes, turning and basting frequently until lightly charred and tender. Serve at once with lemon wedges and mango salsa, if wished.

Serves 4
Preparation time: 15 minutes, plus 1 hour marinading time
Cooking time: 6–8 minutes

MANGO SALSA

½ small ripe mango, peeled, seeded, and diced
1 tablespoon chopped red onion
1 tablespoon chopped cilantro
1 small red chile, seeded and chopped
1 tablespoon dark soy sauce
1 tablespoon lime juice
1 teaspoon clear honey
salt and pepper

Combine all the ingredients in a bowl and season to taste. Chill until required.

57

MONKFISH KEBOBS WITH CUMIN AND MINT

The combination of mint and cumin gives this dish an exotic flavour.

3 pounds monkfish, skinned and filleted
½ cup olive oil
1 tablespoon lemon juice
1 tablespoon cumin seeds, lightly crushed
2 tablespoons finely chopped fresh mint,
lightly pounded, or 1 tablespoon
dried mint
salt and pepper

Dip:
⅔ cup plain yogurt, chilled
1 cucumber, sliced and chopped
mint sprigs, to garnish

1 Cut the monkfish into bite-size cubes and put into a large shallow dish. Combine the oil, lemon juice, cumin seeds, and mint. Season with salt and lots of black pepper, then pour over the fish. Stir to coat, then leave to marinate at room temperature for 1 hour.*

2 Thread the fish on to 6 skewers and grill over a very hot barbecue for 4–5 minutes, turning every minute until just cooked, brushing frequently with the marinade.

3 Mix the yogurt and chopped cucumber, and garnish with mint. Serve immediately, providing the yogurt as a dip, with pita bread and lettuce.

*This dish may be prepared up to 24 hours in advance and kept chilled. Bring to room temperature before cooking.

Serves 6
Preparation time: 10 minutes, plus 1 hour marinading time
Cooking time: 4–5 minutes

MONKFISH KEBOBS

1¼ pounds monkfish tail,
cut into 1-inch cubes
⅔ cup plain yogurt
1 tablespoon black peppercorns,
lightly crushed
3 tablespoons olive oil
18 sage leaves
salt
sage leaves, to garnish
lemon wedges, to serve

1 Place the cubed monkfish in a large bowl with the yogurt, peppercorns, olive oil, and a sprinkling of salt. Stir well and then cover and leave for 1 hour in a cool place, turning occasionally.

2 Remove the monkfish from the marinade, reserving the marinade, and thread the fish on to 4–6 oiled skewers, alternating with the sage leaves. Cook on the oiled grill of a preheated barbecue for 10–15 minutes, basting with the reserved marinade.

3 Garnish with sage leaves and serve with lemon wedges and a cucumber and tomato salad.

Serves 4–6
Preparation time: 15 minutes, plus 1 hour marinading time
Cooking time: 10–15 minutes

FISH KEBOBS WITH HERB BUTTER

8 slices bacon
4 ounces button mushrooms
I pound halibut or cod steaks,
cut in 2-inch cubes
4 tomatoes, quartered
2 green bell peppers, seeded and
cut in chunks
8 ounces orange roughy fillet,
skinned and cut in squares

Herb butter:
¾ stick butter
I tablespoon each finely chopped fresh dill
weed, tarragon, and chives
I tablespoon lemon juice
salt and pepper

1 First make the herb butter. Melt the butter in a small saucepan, add the herbs, lemon juice, and salt and pepper and mix well.
2 Remove the rind from the bacon and roll up each slice. Make up the kebobs by threading the prepared ingredients on to 4 oiled skewers.
3 Brush the kebobs with the herb butter and cook on the barbecue over medium hot coals for about 8–10 minutes, turning and basting 2 or 3 times during cooking.
4 Serve the kebobs with the remaining butter poured over the top.

Serves 4
Preparation time: 10 minutes
Cooking time: 8–10 minutes

PARSLEYED HALIBUT KEBOBS

2 pounds halibut fillet, skinned and cut
into I-inch cubes
I½ sticks butter, softened
¼ teaspoon fennel seeds, finely ground
I teaspoon Anisette or Pernod
I large bunch of parsley, stems discarded
salt and pepper
lemon wedges, to serve (optional)

1 Pat the fish dry with paper towels and reserve.
2 Beat the butter with the fennel seeds and Anisette or Pernod. Thread the fish on to 6 skewers and spread with the fennel butter paste.
3 Chop the parsley very finely, in a food processor if available. Spread all over a flat plate or work surface, and roll the skewers in it, until completely covered. Remove the rack from the broiler pan and place the skewers on it.
4 Cook the fish under a preheated very hot broiler for 5 minutes, turning every minute, until the fish is cooked and the parsley is crisp and dark green. Serve at once, sprinkled with salt and pepper, accompanied by lemon wedges, if wished.

Serves 6
Preparation time: 25 minutes
Cooking time: 5 minutes

60

DEEP SEA SKEWERS

4 bacon slices, rind removed
2 halibut or cod steaks, skinned
and quartered
8 large cooked shrimp, peeled
4 mushrooms
4 tomatoes, halved
watercress sprigs, to garnish

Marinade:
6 tablespoons lemon juice
large pinch of paprika
2 tablespoons corn oil
1 bay leaf
1 parsley sprig
1 small onion, sliced
salt and pepper

1 To make the marinade, combine all the ingredients with salt and pepper to taste in a large shallow bowl.
2 Lay the bacon slices on a board and stretch them with the back of a knife, then cut them in half crosswise. Season the fish pieces, then roll each piece in a slice of bacon and place in the marinade. Add the shrimp and mushrooms and turn carefully to coat. Cover and leave to marinate in the refrigerator, turning from time to time, for about 4 hours.
3 Drain, reserving the marinade. Thread the fish rolls, shrimp, and mushrooms on to 4 oiled kebob skewers with the halved tomatoes, alternating the ingredients. Brush well with the reserved marinade.
4 Cook on a hot barbecue, turning from time to time, and basting with marinade, for about 10 minutes, or until tender. Serve garnished with watercress sprigs.

Serves 4
Preparation time: 15 minutes, plus 4 hours marinading time
Cooking time: 10 minutes

VARIATION
For a special occasion, you could use 8–10 large scallops instead of the fish steaks.

BARBECUED SCALLOPS

24 slices bacon, rind removed
12 large scallops, cleaned and halved
16 bay leaves
lime or lemon wedges, to serve

1 Wrap a slice of bacon around each scallop half and then thread on to oiled metal skewers, alternating with the bay leaves.
2 Cook on the oiled grill of a preheated barbecue for about 8–10 minutes, turning frequently, until the bacon is crisp.
3 Serve with lime or lemon wedges.

Serves 4
Preparation time: 5 minutes
Cooking time: 8–10 minutes

RED SNAPPER AND BACON KEBOBS

I red snapper, about 3 pounds, cleaned,
filleted, and skinned
4 tablespoons olive oil
8 ounces bacon slices, rind removed
2 tablespoons finely chopped sage leaves
1–2 garlic cloves, finely chopped
salt and pepper

1 Cut the red snapper into large slices, place in a bowl and sprinkle with the olive oil.
2 Roll the bacon slices into squares. Pound the sage with the garlic and a good pinch of salt.
3 Thread the fish, reserving the oil, and bacon on to 6 skewers, starting with bacon, using 2 rolls of bacon every now and again, if necessary, between 2 cubes of snapper.
4 Rub a little of the sage and garlic mixture over the fish, then sprinkle with pepper. Sprinkle over the oil.
5 Cook under a preheated very hot broiler for 7–12 minutes, turning every 2 minutes until the fish is cooked and the bacon is crisp. Serve with rice and a green salad.

Serves 6
Preparation time: 15 minutes
Cooking time: 7–12 minutes

BROCHETTE OF FISH WITH HERBS

1½ pounds halibut or monkfish
3 tablespoons olive oil
I tablespoon lemon juice
I tablespoon chopped tarragon
I tablespoon chopped dill weed
I tablespoon chopped parsley
2 lemons, quartered, to serve

1 Skin and bone the fish, cut into neat cubes, and put them in a bowl. Pour over the olive oil and lemon juice, and stir in the chopped herbs. Leave to marinate for 3–4 hours.
2 Thread the cubes of fish on to 4 skewers. Grill slowly under a preheated broiler, turning often and basting with the oil and lemon juice, for about 8 minutes, until the fish is tender and cooked. Serve with lemon quarters.

Serves 4
Preparation time: 5 minutes, plus 3–4 hours marinading time
Cooking time: 8 minutes

INDEX